NETWORK SECURITY

Aiswarya Ram MBA, CCNA

DEDICATION

I dutifully dedicate this work to the powerful
GREAT ALMIGHTY

CONTENTS

NETWORK SECURITY

ACKNOWLEDGMENTS

I acknowledge the GOD ALMIGHTY for enabling me .

1 WHAT IS NETWORK SECURITY

Security is a very, very important thing for us.
As the number of hackers are increasing exponentially, network security is paramount.

What Is Network Security?

Some of the many types of network security available include distributed denial of service (DDoS) attack prevention, firewalls, email gateways, intrusion prevention/detection system (IPS/IDS), security information and event management (SIEM) systems, network access control (NAC), virtual private networks (VPNs), etc.

Network Security in simple, is a set of rules, regulations, protocols, procedures and configurations designed to protect the confidentiality, integrity, and accessibility of networks by means of both software and hardware technologies.

Every institution, regardless of type, size,

segment, industry or infrastructure, necessitates a degree of network security solutions in place to shield it from the encompassing network security threats across the world today.

Today's network architecture is complex and is faced with a threat environment that is always changing and attackers that are always trying to find and exploit vulnerabilities. These vulnerabilities can exist in a broad number of areas, including devices, data, applications, users and locations.

Several network security management tools and applications are in use today to address individual threats.

Some addresses explanation and also regulatory non-compliance.

Now a day, a few minutes of downtime originates widespread disruption and enormous damage to the bottom line and reputation.

It is vital that ample protection measures are in place.

Network security is a fundamental concept that is essential to any government/ company/person using information technology.

This lesson lists a few of the common types of network security systems and describes their role on the network.

One can think of network security as the countermeasures that are implemented on a network to keep the network and data safe from hackers, fraudsters, criminals, and negligent employees. It is most effective when it is implemented in layers. These layers build up a protective defense against all network threats. The idea is that each layer will cast up a detection and/or prevention net which monitors, identifies, alerts, and stops threats to the network.

Network security is the act of protecting files and directories in a network of computers against misuse, hacking, and unauthorized access to the system.
It is designed to protect the usability and integrity of the network and data. It comprises hardware and software AND Effective network security to the network.
It manages access, targets threats and halts them from intruding into your network.
It aims to protect data sent through devices in the network to ensure that the information is not changed/ intercepted.

The network security team implements the hardware and software necessary to guard your security architecture.

By ensuring a proper network security system in place, we can detect emerging threats before they infiltrate into our network and compromise our data.

A lot of components in a network security system work together to mend our security stance.

Network security entails the procedures, protocols,POLICIES and practices approved to thwart and monitor access, misuse, modification, and refutation.

It involves the authorization of access to data in a network, meticulously managed by a network administrator.

Users are assigned an ID & password to authenticate information.

It consents access to information and programs within their right.

Generally, it covers a multiplicity of networks, public and private, employed in everyday jobs/ transactions/communications among businesses/ government/ individuals.

Networks may either be private, such as within an establishment, or others open to public access.

It does as its name enlightens: It secures the network, as well as protecting and overseeing operations to be implemented.

The simplest and common way of protecting a

network is by allocating a unique ID and a corresponding password.

Network security starts with authentication, generally with a username and a password. The one-factor authentication requires just one detail authenticating the user name/ password.

In 2FA, i.e., two factor authentication, the user 'has' is also used, like token/card/smartphone, etc.

3FA, i.e., three factor authentication, uses biometric/ finger print/ retinal scan etc.

After authentication, a firewall administers access policies like what kind of services are allowed to be accessed by the users.

It is operational to prevent unauthorized access, but it may fail to prevent potentially harmful content like Trojans/viruses/worms transmitted to the network.

Anti-virus software or an intrusion prevention system (IPS) help detect and inhibit the action of such malware. An anomaly-based intrusion detection system may also monitor the network logged for audit purposes and for later high-level analysis.

Full network traffic analysis incorporating Machine learning identifies active network attackers from malicious insiders/ targeted external attackers.

encrypted communication between two network hosts upholds data privacy.

essentially decoy network-accessible resources, like honeypots may be positioned in networks for surveillance and early-warning.

honeypots are not customarily retrieved for legitimate purposes.

A honeypot directs an attacker's attention away from legitimate servers.

Techniques used by the attackers to compromise these decoy resources should be deliberated after an attack, to enlighten on new exploitation techniques.

This analysis may be used to further tighten security of the affected network.

The honeypot, distracts attention from the data on the real server to inspire attackers to employ their time and energy on the decoy server.

The honeynet is a network set up with intentional vulnerabilities. Its purpose is to invite attacks so that the attacker's methods can be analyzed and that information to be used to increase network security.

With hackers getting smarter and more frequent as years pass, network security has become more important than ever.

2 HOW DO I GAIN

How do I benefit from network security?

Digitization has transformed the entire contemporary world.
How people live, work, play, and learn have all are mesmerizingly altered.
Every one that desires to deliver the services to customers and employees must protect its network.
Network security also protect proprietary information from attack. It protects the reputation also.

Integrity, Availability and Confidentiality are the major Network Security Goals.
Every network security measures try to address at least one of these 3 targets.

Ensure the availability of data, Protect the confidentiality of data or/and Preserve the integrity of data.

Network security is involved in government, organizations, enterprises, and other types of institutions.

Out of this, Network security is utmost important for any government, as it involves national security also.

As the network needs security against attackers and hackers, what are the key principles of security?

Network Security contains 5 basic securities.

First is the security of data information, Second is computer security to protect data and to thwart hackers, third is Passwords, fourth is Keystroke Monitoring, and fifth is protecting Audit Data.

While Confidentiality regulates the secrecy of the information asset, the

Integrity portion supplies the accurate and reliable data assurance.

Network security is important for government, home networks as well as in the business world.

Most high-speed internet connections have one or more wireless routers, to be exploited if not properly secured.

A compact system of network security helps reduce the risk of data loss, theft and sabotage.

Who is accountable for network security in place?

Human resources department is responsible for awareness training and campaigns.

Developers needs to develop new apps, technology, and products with security in mind.
CEO is accountable and responsible for ensuring appropriate procedures, policies, protocols and reporting practices.

Network security is the most important types of security you should have which will work to protect the usability and integrity of your network and data.
Network security works by identifying and targeting all kinds of attacks and threats, then stops them from entering and affecting your network.
Network security is your own personal, data protection wall.

How Network Security Works?

Multiple layers of defenses at the edge and in the network are there to consider when addressing

network security throughout an organization.
Attacks happen at any layer.
Your network security configuration, LAN, WAN, hardware, software, procedures, processes and policies are bound to be intended to address each area.

Every network security layer executes policies, procedures, protocols, processes and controls.
Authorized users enter access to network.
Malicious people are blocked from carrying out exploits and threats.

Network security typically involves of 6 different controls, viz., administrative, physical, technical, Preventative, Detective, and Responsive.
Here is a brief description of the different types of network security and how each control works.

Administrative control:
Administrative controls involve security policies, procedures, protocols, and processes that control user activities, counting how users are authenticated, their level of access and how IT staff members implement changes to the infrastructure.

Physical control:

Physical controls, designed to prevent unauthorized people from gaining physical access to network components such as switches, routers, cabling, cupboards, etc.

Controlled access, such as user name, password, codes, locks, finger print, biometric authentication, etc. are sine qua non in any organization.

Technical control

Technical controls protect data stored on the network.

It also controls and protect data in transit into or out of the network.

The 2-fold protection needs to protect data and systems from unauthorized people, and against malicious activities from employees.

documented processes and countermeasures such as firewalls must be applied for the purposes of security.

The role of network security is to protect the IT infrastructure from all types of threats including:

- Hackers
- Trojan
- Worms
- Viruses
- Zero-day attacks
- Hacker attacks
- Denial of service attacks

- Spyware
- adware

The most common network security components include:
- Anti-virus software
- Virtual private networks (VPN)
- Firewalls
- Intrusion detection systems(IDS)
- Intrusion prevention systems(IPS)

When network security is compromised, our first priority should be to get the attackers out as quickly as possible. The longer they keep in your network; the longer they need to steal your non-public information.

According to Ponemon Institute's 2013 Cost of Data Breach study, excluding catastrophic or mega data security breaches, the average cost of a data breach per compromised record in the U.S. is $188. The average total cost to an organization in the U.S. is more than $5.4 million.

The most effective method of lessening the total cost is by getting the attackers out of your network as soon as possible.

3 TYPES

There are various types of network security, such as Application security, Network Access Control, Antivirus and Antimalware Software, Email Security, Wireless Security, VPN_Virtual Private Networks, Behavioral analytics, DLP_ Data loss prevention, SIEM_ Security information and event management, etc.

NAC_Network Access Control

NAC decides and manage who can and can't access the network by distinguishing which devices and users are allowed into the network.
From there, you can enforce various security policies such as blocking certain devices and controlling what someone can do within your network.
You can also utilize behavioral analytic tools to identify what normal and abnormal behavior is.
Once you are doing that, you will set it up wherever you'll get notifications whenever one

thing is acting abnormally.

Similarly, you will implement firewalls, that is after you place a barrier between your internal network and untrusted outside networks, like the web.

This way, you will conjointly manage your staff's net use and block any threats or dangerous websites.

Not each user ought to have access to your network. To stay out potential attackers, you would like to acknowledge every user and every device. Then you will enforce your security policies. You will block noncompliant endpoint devices or offer them solely restricted access. This method process is NAC.

To ensure that potential attackers cannot infiltrate your network, comprehensive access management policies have to be compelled to be in situ for each users and devices. It can be set at the foremost granular level.

for instance, you may grant full access to the network, however deny access to specific confidential folders or stop their personal devices from joining the connection.

Application Security
Application security is strictly however it sounds

– security that protects your applications. this sort of security is vital to own as a result of no app is made utterly.

They will have a great deal of holes or weaknesses wherever a hacker will enter.

Any code you utilize to run your business must be protected, whether or not your IT employees builds it or whether or not you get it. sadly, any application might contain holes, or vulnerabilities, that attackers will use to infiltrate your network. Application security encompasses the hardware, software, and processes you utilize to shut those holes.

A lot of your business operations and devices might run on applications, therefore this sort of security could be a must-have.

Antivirus and Antimalware code

Antivirus and Antimalware
This code is employed to shield against malware, which has something from viruses, Trojans, ransomware, or spyware.

viruses, worms, Trojanhorses, ransomware, spyware, etc. are examples of Malicious software.

Generally, malware can infect a network however lie dormant for days or perhaps weeks.

An anti-malware not only scan for malware upon entry, but also continuously track files afterward to find anomalies, remove malware, and fix damage.

Besides the apparent reasons, malware may be terribly dangerous as a result of generally, it will can keep calm inside your network for days and weeks, simply sitting there able to develop and attack.

Antivirus and antimalware software package shield a company from a variety of malicious software package, as well as viruses, ransomware, worms and trojans. the most effective software package not solely scans files upon entry to the network however unendingly scans and tracks files.

Antivirus and antimalware software package handle this threat by scanning for malware entry and following files later on to seek out any that will have slipped in and area unit birth low.

Email Security
Here's a giant one. Your email is pretty vital for your business.
Considering that email gateways are the pathway

for a security breach, email security is an absolute vital one to have.

Attackers will use your personal data to try and do all types of harm, like blackmail or emailing on your behalf to deceive your shoppers and send them to sites jam-packed with malware. Email gateways area unit the amount one threat vector for a security breach. Attackers use personal data and social engineering techniques to create subtle phishing campaigns to deceive recipients and send them to sites serving up malware. associate email security application blocks incoming attacks and controls departing messages to stop the loss of sensitive knowledge.

An email security application will facilitate block these attacks and management what's sent out.

Wireless Security

The mobile workplace movement is gaining momentum, and thereupon comes wireless networks and access points. Wireless networks aren't as secure as wired ones. while not tight security measures, putting in a wireless LAN is like putt local area network ports all over, together with the parking zone.

To prevent an exploit from taking hold, you need products specifically designed to protect a wireless network.

However, wireless networks aren't as secure as wired ones, permitting a lot of area for hacker entry, that the power of wireless security must be robust.

Since there are several components to your infrastructure, there are many sorts of security out there to safeguard it.

There are a lot more that I didn't mention here.

I welcome you to contact me to get more information on how to get started on your own, custom secure system.

4 HOW TO SECURE

Now let's take a look at some of the different ways you can secure your network.

Firewall
Firewall Protection act as a barrier between the untrusted external networks and your trusted internal network.
Firewalls place up a barrier between your trusty internal network and untrusted outside networks, like the web. They use a collection of outlined rules to permit or block traffic. A firewall will be hardware, software, or both.

Administrators usually assemble a collection of outlined rules that blocks or permits traffic onto the network.
A protection should provide seamless and centrally managed management of network traffic, whether or not it's physical, virtual or within the cloud.
VPN_Virtual non-public Networks

VPN could be a software system application that is primary purpose is to code on-line information traffic. 1stdeveloped for business protection functions, over the years VPN suppliers developed applications for private use. to boot, VPN masks and changes informatics address, and could be a widespread tool for bypassing Geoblocking.

Some VPNs additionally provide server obfuscation services, adBlocks, and disables trackers.

Virtual non-public networks (VPNs) produce a affiliation to the network from another termination or website. for instance, users functioning from home would usually connect with the organization's network over a VPN. information between the 2 points is encrypted and also the user would want to demonstrate to permit communication between their device and also the network.

It ought to organize organizations to quickly produce VPNs drag-and-drop and to safeguard all locations with our Next Generation Firewall answer.

Behavioral analytics

To discover abnormal network behavior, you need to grasp what traditional behavior sounds like. Behavior analytics tools mechanically tell apart activities that deviate from the norm. Your security team will then higher establish indicators of compromise that create a possible downside and quickly amend threats.

DLP_Data loss hindrance

Organizations should check that that their workers don't send sensitive info outside the network. Information loss hindrance, or DLP, technologies will stop folks from uploading, forwarding, or maybe printing essential info in AN unsafe manner.

IPS_ intrusion prevention system

An intrusion prevention system (IPS) scans network traffic to actively block attacks. NGIPS appliances do this by correlating huge amounts of global threats.

It not solely blocks malicious activity however additionally track the progression of suspect files and malware across the network to forestall the unfold of outbreaks and reinfection.

Network criminals ar progressively targeting mobile devices and apps. among successive three years, ninety p.c of IT organizations could support company applications on personal mobile devices. Of course, you would like to manage that devices will access your network. you may additionally ought to assemble their connections to stay network traffic personal.

Software-defined segmentation puts network traffic into totally different classifications. Ideally, the classifications ar supported termination identity, not mere information processing addresses. you'll be able to assign access rights supported role, location, and additional so the correct level of access is given to the correct individuals and suspicious devices ar contained and remediated.

SIEM_Security data and event management

SIEM product garner the knowledge that your staff must establish and reply to threats. These products are available varied forms, as well as physical and virtual appliances and server code.

A virtual personal network encrypts the affiliation from associate termination to a network, typically over the web. Typically, a remote-access VPN uses IPsec or Secure Sockets Layer to certify the communication between device and network. net| internet|online security resolution can management your staff's web use, block web-based threats, and deny access to malicious websites. it'll shield your net entree on website or within the cloud.

Use technologies such as a next-generation firewall (NGFW) or an intrusion prevention system (IPS).

Segment network access

Limit the resources that an attacker can access. By dynamically dominant access in the least times, you facilitate make sure that your entire network isn'tcompromised in a very single attack.

Keep an in depth eye on network activity

Being able to visualize everything happening across your network and information center will assist you uncover attacks that bypass the perimeter. Deploy a zone (DMZ) or add a layer of security to your native space network (LAN).

Prevent initial infiltration

Most ransomware infections occur through Associate in Nursing email attachment or a malicious transfer.

Arm your endpoints

Antivirus solutions on your endpoints don't satisfy any longer.

Set up privileges so they perform tasks such as granting the appropriate network shares or user permissions on endpoints. Two-factor authentications will also help.

Gain real-time threat intelligence

Know your enemy. Take advantage of threat intelligence from organizations such as Talos to understand security information and emerging network security threats.

Say no to ransom

Never, ever pay the ransom. There's no guarantee you'll get your data back, and you're only fueling the network criminals for more attacks.

5 WHO IS RESPONSIBLE

Who is responsible for the network security of your data/ government/ Company?

Many firms hold IT alone chargeable for on-line data privacy and security.

Experts argue it is not a sustainable security business model.

Internet space is the largest ungoverned space in recorded human history.

there is no online rule-of-law.

If the government is unable to protect their own information, citizens and businesses would not wait for the government.

 You need to do it yourself.

However, it looks that for several businesses, security remains an afterthought.

Companies generally rely solely on their IT team to champion network security and information privacy efforts.

This poses a conflict of interest, leaving network security as a second-string priority.

It is better to segregate out the expenditure on

security as a discrete part of the overall spend in the company.

the problem currently lies for many businesses are no-segregation.

If the whole network security budget lies in the hands of IT, it's likely that they will fully invest in tools, then solely rely on those tools for information security.

This inclination comes strictly from their business objectives.

It is IT's job to innovate, maintain user-friendly interfaces, and ensure employees have the necessary access to important files and apps, enhancing productivity.

They conjointly have to be compelled to foster collaboration and information sharing.

All these, and any company-specific business objectives build security quite low on IT's list of priorities.

With security low on the priority list, it's clear that it's going to not be the simplest department to carry possession of such an important, complete business objective.

In such a situation World Health Organization is responsible?

Before diving into the blame game, it's vital that we tend to build a distinction between responsibility and answerableness.

With this understanding, it's vital that whereas it's

answerable for following network security policies and procedures set forth by the corporate, they cannot be command answerable for each breach or incident.

THEN, who?

Keeping the difference between responsibility and accountability in mind, everyone in the government/ company IS responsible for network security.

Eighty percent of the professionals from data protection and privacy training reports their employees are the weakest link in their efforts to create a strong security posture.

This may be partly as a result of corporation's square measure relying thus heavily on that while not giving personal responsibility to each worker, furthermore as militarization them with the information and resources to require responsibility upon themselves.

Tools are an awfully vital ingredient.

Firewalls, antivirus software, and machine learning mechanisms will create effective protections for your network, but with 65% of threats coming from internally, these tools are

just not enough.
Everyone has to take responsibility for his or her data security practices.

Human resources department should be responsible for awareness training and campaigns.

Developers needs to develop new apps, technology, and products with security in mind. Group heads are the accountable ones and are responsible for ensuring appropriate policies, protocols and reporting practices are in place. Marketing team should be responsible for making those policies and protocols widely known throughout the organization.

The security team has to develop policies and protocols in conjunction with the manager team, superintend access rights, perform regular penetration tests, and choose/create security tools, furthermore as produce incident response plans, iteration into that spoken language.

As the cat is already out-of-the-bag on the Board holding accountability.

This should be a no-brainer as a large security breach/incident doesn't only affect finances and productivity, but can severely damage customers' trust towards the brand.

This plan of shared responsibility depends on an organization culture that values security.

Company culture is always set from the top, which is why it's important for the biggest champions of security.

It need to advocate for this culture to establish clear communication with executives around security issues and make businesses cases for the importance of security measures.

If executives square measure willing to carry answerableness regarding security problems, everybody else within the company ought to hold responsibility for his or her individual and division security.

For security consultants wanting to advance security interests, produce additional awareness and boost security as a mainstay of company culture; hopefully, you'll be able to use some points made public during this post to assist build the business case for approaching your government team.

Laws and rules can probably ne'er catch up to the fast growth of technological advances, thus it's in our hands to make sure that security becomes prime of mind for everybody in our corporations. As our on-line lives become additional comprehensive, they conjointly become a larger risk to our personal safety and also the safety of our workers.

We all understand risk issue is often there in everything we tend to do.

We can solely watch out of, a way to defend ourselves before any worst issue on our personal issue happens.

6 CIA TRIAD

Experts developing policies and procedures for an effective information security program, use the CIA triad as a guide.

The CIA stands for Confidentiality, Integrity and Availability. Confidentiality ensures information is inaccessible to unauthorized people.

It is enforced through encryption in many formats.

Integrity protects the information and systems from being altered by unauthorized elements.

Integrity ensures the data is accurate and trustworthy.

Availability ensures licensed folks will access the data once required which all hardware and code maintained properly and updated once necessary.

The independent CIA triad has become the de facto normal model for keeping your organization secure.

These are the3 fundamental principles help build a vigorous set of security controls to preserve and protect your data.

Network security is delivered in three ways that embody the employment of a hardware appliance, software, or a cloud service.

Hardware appliances are special servers or network equipment that perform a specific network security function.

They can be installed on the network out of the direct path of network traffic (out-of-line), but they are most commonly installed in the direct line of network traffic (in-line).

When appliances are in-line, they can stop security threats, instead of just monitoring and alerting you about them.

Special network security software can be installed on servers or PCs to enable network protection functions.

The most important areas of focus I identified are as follows:

2-FA Two-Factor Authentication

Two-factor authentication should always be enabled.

Systems Integration & Cohesive Security Architecture:

Businesses today need to integrate systems and create a cohesive security architecture.

Ensure the systems you are supposed to be monitoring are integrated and enabling automated responses.

Training &Awareness:

Security needs to be a priority for everyone, regardless of role.

Training, education, and awareness around phishing attacks are a critical way to reduce the risk of stolen credentials.

Visibility is critically important to the successful

execution of digital transformation. Simply put, you can't defend what you can't see.

Effectively Introducing Automation into Threat-mediation:

Better visibility into different parts of the security environment is becoming more widely available, but there are still many moving parts that are shifting constantly.

Automation can make remediation for known vulnerabilities more efficient let you contain security threats with higher confidence.

Security Before Design and Deployment:

Leaders need to ensure that security is a continual, and iterative design process between IT, Security and Citizen Developers who together aim to achieve a common goal.

Your Security Strategy target to Continually Advance Effectiveness.

The end state of digital transformation shifts continuously; understanding this is key to future-proofing security strategy. The right security strategy should anticipate the needs of a business as table stakes.

Security to be Part of Business Nomenclature at the Top.

Network security is a C-level conversation. Driving revenue growth and richer client interactions while reducing business risk is a shared objective across all leaders and must be communicated to all employees as such.

Security Strategy to Evolve with the Business: Technology and security change quickly, so security strategies must be revisited regularly.

It needs to be a constant reevaluation process with periodic adjustments depending on both the changing direction of the business and technological advances.

Vulnerability Patching is of equal importance to maintain a timely vulnerability-patching program that is indexed onto the highest threats that are coming in relative to your organization.

Digital transformation is inevitable in the modern world.

The success of any organization's digital transformation relies on their attitude to tackling a world where network security threats are pervasive.

Organizations face many difficulties implementing the above but while these actions do take time and come with challenges, they enable conversation.

7 SOCIAL ENGINEERING

When network threat actors target you, they research not only your business, but your employees.

Because human element is the weakest link in any environment.

They know that employees outside of IT security aren't as aware of network threats, so they execute network attacks that exploit human vulnerabilities.

Through the process of social engineering, threat actors manipulate people into giving the access to sensitive information.

The most common social engineering attacks, inter alia, include Baiting, Phishing, Pretexting, Quid pro quo, etc.

When a threat actor requests personal data in

exchange for a few type of reward, i.e. money, free gift or a free service, that is called Quid pro quo.

When a threat actor impersonates an authority figure or someone that the target would easily trust in order to get their personal information, it is Pretexting.

Phishing is usually in the form of emails/ chats, where the threat actors pose as a real organization to obtain personal information.

On the other hand, Baiting is when threat actors leave a malware-infected device, such as a USB or CD, in a place where it can be easily found by someone, who would then use the infected device on their laptop and accidentally install the malware, giving the threat actors access into the target's system.

As a business leader, it is your responsibility to build a culture of security awareness and fill in the gaps in your team's network security knowledge and understanding.

It's essential that your workforce be informed of network security risks, so it will be less likely for an employee to fall victim to an attack.

Strengthen your organization's human firewall and mitigate the possibility of a network attack, to treat the Cause, Not the Symptom.

Keeping pace with online threats can often feel like you're plugging holes in a dam with your fingers.

As employers create more flexible work conditions and mobility increases, organizations are faced with an increasingly complex task of the corporate network.

This is why the flexibility to speedily sight wicked activity once associate soul has physical access to a digital computer is therefore vital.

With physical access, associate soul might transfer knowledge to a USB device, associate external Winchester drive or mobile phone/threat actors might use these commonplace quality devices to infect your network with malware.

Getting to the Root of a Vulnerability is traditional security controls like firewalls and antivirus software can alert you if you've been infected with malware.

But they don't offer the visibility required to detect crucial elements in the lifecycle of this kind of breach.

Without the flexibility see wherever the infection originated, your security team can be centered on treating symptoms and not the basis cause.

Don't Let Devices Lead to Downfall as Mobility has made USB devices commonplace in the workplace and many remain unaware of the risks these seemingly benign tools present.

Having tools and the right expertise to interpret and correlate the data is critical to combat issues of compromise.

But be sure you're practicing strong end point security using

1.Limit access to administrative privileges,

2.help prevent Shadow IT by limiting administrative rights that allow employees to use programs that have not been vetted by your IT and security teams,

3.Implement and enforce a strict USB user policy,

4.There are solutions to help enforce USB policy.

5. An Active Directory Group Policy Object can allow read access but prevent write access, preventing it from copying information from the end user's drive,

6.Conduct regular security awareness training for employees at all levels, and

7.Threat actors know they can exploit human vulnerabilities so keep security top of mind and arm your staff with strategies to prevent compromise.

The physical and digital world are nearly indistinguishable nowadays. Even more amazing is the speed at which the divide has closed, and the overlap has begun.

If you think about the fact it took nearly one hundred years for the first industrial revolution to give way to mass production, it feels like the fourth industrial revolution has come about at lightning speed.

While the adoption of technology in our everyday lives and in industry brings many advantages, it does need to come with a caveat.

Businesses should naturally embrace digital transformation, but they must do it securely.

The last twenty years is a great use case about society's lack of foresight when it comes to the dangers that digital transformation can pose to our world.

Viruses such as 'Witty Worm' in 2004, 'Zeus' in 2007, 'Stuxnet' in 2010, 'Cryptolocker' in 2013, and more recently the 'WannaCry ransomware' attack in 2017 show just how damaging lack of preparedness can be.

8 PROTECT YOURSELF

How to protect yourself from ransomware?

There are several ways to protect yourself from ransomware.

Back up all your data

In the event of an attack, you'll power down the end point, reimage it, and put in your recent backup.

You'll have all of your information and you'll forestall the ransomware from spreading to different systems.

Patch your systems

Make a habit of change your code frequently. Fixing unremarkably exploited third-party code can foil several attacks.

Educate users on attack sources

The weakest link within the security chain is typically human.

Empower them to not fall for phishing or different schemes.

Protect your network

Take a bedded approach, with security infused from the end point to email to the DNS layer.

Malware protection

Malware is intrusive code that's designed to wreck and destroy PCs and computer systems.

Malware could be a contraction for "malicious code." samples of common malware includes viruses, worms, Trojan viruses, spyware, adware, and ransomware.

How do I defend my network against malware?

Typically, businesses target preventative tools to prevent breaches.

By securing the perimeter, businesses assume they're safe.

Some advanced malware, however, can eventually create their approach into your network.

As a result, it's crucial to deploy technologies that frequently monitor and find malware that has evaded perimeter defenses.

Sufficient advanced malware protection needs multiple layers of safeguards alongside high-level network visibility and intelligence.

How do I find and reply to malware?

Malware can inevitably penetrate your network. you want to have defenses that give vital visibility and breach detection.

so as to get rid of malware, you want to be able to establish malicious actors quickly.

This needs constant network scanning.

Once the threat is known, you want to take away the malware from your network.

Today's antivirus merchandise isn't enough to shield against advanced network threats.

Malware varieties

Virus

Viruses are a subgroup of malware.

A pandemic is malicious code hooked up to a document or file that supports macros to execute its code and unfold from host to host.

Once downloaded, the virus can lay dormant till the file is opened and in use.

Viruses are designed to disrupt a system's ability to work.

As a result, viruses will cause vital operational problems and information loss.

Worms

Worms are malicious code that apace replicates and spreads to any device inside the network.

Not like viruses, worms don't want host programs to bare.

A worm infects a tool via a downloaded file or a network association before it multiplies and disperses at an exponential rate.

Like viruses, worms will severely disrupt the operations of a tool and cause information loss.

Trojan virus

Trojan viruses are disguised as useful code programs.

However, once the user downloads it, the Trojan virus will gain access to sensitive information then modify, block, or delete the info.

This may be extraordinarily harmful to the performance of the device.

Not like traditional viruses and worms, Trojan viruses aren't designed to self-replicate.

Spyware

Spyware is malicious code that runs on the Q.T. on a pc and reports back to a distant user.

Instead of merely disrupting a device's operations, spyware targets sensitive info and may grant remote access to predators.

Spyware is commonly accustomed steal monetary or personal info.

A selected kind of spyware could be a key logger, that records your keystrokes to reveal passwords and private info.

Adware

Adware is malicious code accustomed collect information on your pc usage and supply applicable advertisements to you.

Whereas adware isn't continuously dangerous, in some cases adware will cause problems for your system.

Adware will direct your browser to unsafe sites, and it will even contain Trojan horses and spyware.

In addition, vital levels of adware will prevent your system perceptibly.

As a result of not all adware is malicious, it's necessary to own protection that perpetually and showing intelligence scans these programs.

Ransomware

Ransomware is malicious code that gains access to sensitive info inside a system, encrypts that info in order that the user cannot access it, then demands a monetary payout for the info to be free.

Ransomware is often a part of a phishing scam.

By clicking a disguised link, the user downloads the ransomware.

The offender payoff to encipher specific info which will solely be opened by a mathematical key they apprehend.

Once the offender receives payment, the info is unbolted.

Fileless malware

It is a kind of memory-resident malware.

Because the term suggests, it's malware that operates from a victim's computer's memory, not from files on the disk drive.

As a result of there are not any files to scan, it's tougher to find than ancient malware.

It additionally makes forensics harder as a result of the malware disappears once the victim pc is rebooted.

In late 2017, the Cisco Talos threat intelligence team announced example of fileless malware that they know as DNS Messenger.

9 MANAGEMENT

Network Security Management

Security management for networks is totally different for all types of things.

A home or little workplace could solely need basic security whereas massive businesses could need high-maintenance and advanced computer code and hardware to stop malicious attacks from hacking and spamming.

Networks area unit subject to attacks from malicious sources.

Attacks is from two classes: Passive and Active.

Passive attack is once a network interloper intercepts knowledge traveling through the network.

Active attack is once associate interloper initiates

commands to disrupt the network's traditional operation.

Otherwise to conduct intelligence and lateral movement to search out and gain access to assets obtainable via the network.

Passive attacks, inter alia, embody Network based mostly wire sound, phone sound, Port scanner, idle scan, encryption, traffic analysis, etc.

Active attacks, inter alia, embody DNS spoofing, DOS attack, knowledge modification, eavesdropping, virus, man within the middle, Arp poisoning, VLAN hopping, smurf attack,buffer overflow, heap overflow, FSA format string attack, SQL injection, CSRF, cross web site scripting, network attack, phishing, etc.

Malicious computer code

Short type of malicious computer code is termed malware.

An online user is treed , tricked or forced into downloading computer code that's of malicious to a system .

Such computer code comes in several forms, like

viruses, worms, spyware, Trojan horses, etc. it's used to disrupt operation.

It gathers sensitive info. It gains access to non-public pc systems.

Malware is outlined by its malicious content and intent, acting against the wants of the pc user, and doesn't embody computer code that causes unintentional hurt because of some deficiency.

A term badware is typically used, and applied to each really malicious computer code and unintentional harmful computer code.

Botnet-network confiscated by a mechanism or larva that performs large-scale malicious acts for the creator is termed a botnet.

Viruses area unit programs that replicate their structures or effects by infecting alternative files or structures on a pc.

The common use of an endemic is to steal knowledge.

Worms area unit programs that may replicate themselves throughout an electronic network, perform malicious tasks throughout.

Ransomeware could be a form of malware that restricts access to the pc system that it infects, and demands a ransom paid to the creator of the malware for the restriction to be removed.

Scareware is scam computer code of typically restricted or no profit, containing malicious payloads, that's sold-out to shoppers via sure unethical promoting practices.

The commercialism approach uses social engineering to cause shock, anxiety, or the perception of a threat, usually directed at associate unsuspecting user.

Spyware is programs that sneakily monitor activity on a system and report that info to others while not the user's consent.

Keylogging could be a quite spyware, typically observed as keylogging or keyboard capturing.
It is that the action of recording /logging the keys affected on keyboard.

A Trojan, could be a general term for malicious computer code that pretends to be harmless, so a user volition ally permits it to be downloaded onto the pc.

DDOS attacks

DDoS (Distributed Denial-of-Service) attack is an effort to create a pc resource unobtainable to its supposed users.

Another way of understanding DDoS is seeing it as attacks that are growing due to the essential characteristics of cloud computing.

Although the means to carry out, motives for, and targets of a DoS attack may vary, it generally consists of the concerted efforts to prevent from functioning efficiently or at all, temporarily or indefinitely.

According to an international business security survey, 25% of respondents experienced a DoS attack in 2007 and 16.8% experienced one in 2010.

DoS attacks often use bots or botnet to carry out the attack.

PHISHING

Phishing attack targets online users for extraction of their sensitive information such as username, password and credit card information.

Phishing happens once the offender pretends to be a trustworthy entity, either via email or online page.

Victims are directed to fake web pages, which are dressed to look legitimate, via spoof emails, instant messenger/social media or other avenues.

Often Email spoofing tactics are used to make emails appear to be from legitimate senders, or long complex domains hide the real website host. Phishing losses came down from $10.8 billion in2016 to $9 billion in 2018 Worldwide.

Application vulnerabilities

Applications accustomed to access net resources could contain security vulnerabilities like blemished authentication checks or memory bugs.
The most severe of those bugs will offer network attackers full management over the pc.
Most security applications and suites area unit incapable of adequate defense against these forms of attacks.

10 FIREWALLS

FIREWALL controls access between networks.

It usually consists of gateways and filters that vary from one firewall to a different.

Firewalls additionally screen network traffic and area unit ready to block traffic that's dangerous.

Firewalls act because the intermediate server between HTTP_ machine-readable text transfer protocol and SMTP connections.

Firewalls impose restrictions on incoming and outgoing network knowledge to and from non-public networks.

Incoming or outgoing traffic should go through the firewall; solely licensed traffic is allowed to go through it.

Firewalls produce checkpoints between an interior non-public network and also the public web, additionally called choke points.

It is the military term of a combat limiting geographical feature.

Firewalls will produce choke points supported informatics supply and protocol port range.

They will additionally function the platform for IPsec.
In victimization tunnel mode capability, firewall is won't to implement VPNs.

Firewalls may also limit network exposure by concealment the interior network system and data from the general public web.

Different types of firewall

Packet filter

A packet filter could be a first generation firewall that processes network traffic on a packet-by-packet basis.

Its main job is to filter traffic from a far off informatics host, therefore a router is required to attach the interior network to the web.

The router is understood as screening router, that

screens packets going and getting into the network.

Stateful packet scrutiny

In a stateful firewall, circuit level entry could be a proxy server that operates at the network level of associate OSI_ open system interconnection model and statically defines what traffic are going to be allowed.

Circuit proxies can forward network packets (formatted unit of knowledge) containing a given port range, if the port is permissible by the rule.

The main advantage of a proxy server is its ability to supply international organization network access translation, which may hide the user's informatics address from the web, effectively protective all internal info from the web.

ALG_ applications level entry

ALG could be a third generation firewall wherever a proxy server operates at the terribly prime of the OSI model, the informatics suite application level.

A network packet is forwarded provided that an association is established employing a celebrated protocol.

Application-level gateways area unit notable for analyzing entire messages instead of individual packets of knowledge once the info area unit being sent or received.

Browser security selection

Web browser statistics tend to have an effect on the number a browser is exploited.
For instance, web someone, that wont to own a majority of the net browser market share, is taken into account very insecure as a result of vulnerabilities were exploited because of its former quality.

According to Wikimedia, Since browser selection is currently additional equally distributed google chrome forty fifth, safari 25%, web someone 6 June 1944, firefox 5%, edge 1.7%, opera 1.3% then on, vulnerabilities are unexploited in many various browsers.

Internet security programs and antivirus computer code will shield a programmable device from attack by detection and eliminating malware.

Antivirus computer code was chiefly package within the early years of the web, however there are units currently many free security applications on the web to decide on from for all platforms.

Password managers

It is a unit of computer code application that facilitate a user store and organize passwords.

It typically store passwords encrypted, requiring the user to make a master password: one, ideally terribly sturdy countersign that grants the user access to their entire countersign info from prime to bottom.

Security suites

McAfee 1st offered the therefore known as security suites purchasable in 2003.

It had a collection of firewalls, antivirus, and opposing spyware, stealing protection, moveable device safety check, non-public web browsing, opposing spam cloud, file device, responsive popup windows) and additional freed from charge.

Network Security for Businesses and shoppers
Network security ought to be a high priority for
any organization that works with networked
knowledge and systems.

Additionally, to protective assets and also the
integrity of knowledge from external exploits,
network security may also manage network traffic
additional with efficiency, enhance network
performance and guarantee secure knowledge
sharing between workers and knowledge sources.

There are several tools, applications and utilities
obtainable that may assist you to secure your
networks from attack and reserve period of time.

Forcepoint offers a collection of network security
solutions typically advanced processes and
guarantee sturdy network security is in situ across
your enterprise.

11 THEFT

A Brief Introduction to Computer Network Security invariably points to the essential necessity to protect your equipment, devices, and data from theft.

Although network security technology improves and evolves because the ways for each attack and defense grow additional subtle, it's higher to implement a number of security basics to any defend your privacy and information.

Security is a necessary facet of networking, and no single method will safeguard networks totally against intruders;

Security needs a mix of approaches.

Physical network security

One unnoted component of network security involves protective hardware devices from stealing and physical intrusion.

Corporations lock network switches and servers, and other core network components in well-guarded facilities.

These measures are not sensible for owners, however you'll keep your password-protected broadband routers in a very personal location, removed from neighbors and houseguests.

If the chance of knowledge stealing through physical suggests that — stealing a pc or router — could be a concern, one answer is to not store your information domestically.
Cloud storage sites and on-line backup sites store sensitive files offsite at secure backup locations.
Even the hardware is taken or compromised, the files remain secure.

Widespread use of mobile devices makes physical security necessary.

Smartphones fall out of pockets, are easy to leave behind, and are stolen.

A few precautions that will keep your devices safe are:

1. Be alert to your physical surroundings whenever you use mobile devices and put them away when you're finished.

2. If your device supports software that allows you to track the device or remotely erase its data, activate it, and use a password with the device to prevent a coworker or acquaintance from looking at your files when you're out of the room.

3. Stay in visual contact with your phone if you loan it to someone.

4. A malicious person can steal personal data, install monitoring software, or otherwise hack a phone in just a few minutes when it's left unattended.

Password Protection

If applied properly, passwords ar extraordinarily effective in rising network security.

Take password management seriously, and don't use weak, easy-to-guess passwords such as abcd123456789.

A few different best practices in positive

identification management go a protracted approach toward network and device security:

1.   Set passcodes on all devices that join the network.
2.   network routers should change the default administrator set passwords.
3.   Don't share passwords with others unless absolutely necessary.
4.   Set up access for friends and visitors, separate as guest window, if possible.
5.   Change passwords frequently, especially if you've shared them or they've been discovered.
6.   Store passwords in a password manager, to make it easier to find and use passwords.

Spyware

Even while not physical access to a tool or knowing any network passwords, illicit programs like spyware will infect computers and networks.

This happens when malicious websites are visited accidentally or through a link in a phishing email.

Spyware takes many forms.

Some varieties monitor pc usage and web-browsing habits to report the info to firms, UN agency then use it to form targeted advertising.

Other kinds of spyware commit to steal personal information.

One of the most dangerous forms of spyware is keylogger software.

It logs and sends the history of all keyboard actions, capturing passwords and credit card numbers along the way.

All spyware tries to perform while not the data of anyone UN agency uses the infected pc, thereby motion a considerable security risk to the pc and therefore the network to that it's connected.

Because spyware is tough to find and take away, security specialists advocate putting in and running reputable anti- spyware code on pc networks.

Online privacy

Personal stalkers and identity thieves monitor people's on-line habits and movements well on the far side the scope of basic spyware.

Wi-Fi hotspot usage on commuter trains and cars reveal your location, for instance.

Even within the virtual world, a lot of a few person's identities are often half-track on-line through the informatics addresses of their networks and their social network activities.

Privacy protection tools include anonymously web proxy servers and VPN services.

Though maintaining complete privacy online is not fully achievable, those methods protect privacy to a certain degree.

Always Be careful what you share online and with whom.

12 REMEDIES

Internet Protocol Security (IPsec)

It is designed to protect TCP/IP communication in a secure manner.

It is a group of security extensions developed by the web task force.
It provides security and authentication at the informatics layer by remodeling knowledge victimization cryptography.

2 main types of transformation that form the basis of IPsec are AH authentication header and ESP.

These 2 protocols provide data integrity, data origin authentication, and anti-replay service.

These protocols can be used alone or in combination to provide the desired set of security services for the network security layer.

The basic elements of the IPsec security design

area unit represented in terms of the subsequent functionalities:

1. Security protocols for AH and clairvoyance

2. Security association for policy management and traffic process

3. Manual and automatic key management for the IKE_ web key exchange.

4. Algorithms for cryptography & authentication

The set of security services provided at the informatics layer includes access management, knowledge origin integrity, protection against replays, and confidentiality.

The rule permits these sets to figure severally while not poignant alternative components of the implementation.
The informatics security implementation is operated in an exceedingly host or security entry atmosphere protectively to IP traffic.

SECURITY TOKEN

Some on-line sites supply customers the power to use a six-digit code that haphazardly changes each 30–60 seconds on a SECURITY TOKEN. The keys on the protection token have inbuilt mathematical computations and manipulate numbers supported the present time designed into the device.

This implies that each thirty seconds there's solely a precise array of numbers potential which might be correct to validate access to the web account.

The web site that the user is work into would be created responsive to that device's serial range and would grasp the computation and proper time designed into the device to verify that the amount given is so one amongst the few six-digit numbers that works therein given 30-60 second cycle.

After 30–60 seconds the device will present a new random six-digit number which can log into the website.

Email security

Email messages are unit composed, delivered,

and hold on in an exceedingly multiple step method, that starts with the message's composition. once the user finishes composing the message and sends it, the message is reworked into a typical format.
Afterwards, the message is transmitted.

Using a network connection, the mail client, referred to as an MUA mail user agent,
connects to an MTA mail transfer agent operating on the mail server.

The mail shopper then provides the sender's identity to the server.
Next, the mail server commands sends the recipient list to the mail server.

The consumer then provides the message.

Once the mail server receives and processes the message, many events occur: recipient server identification, association institution, and message transmission.

Using DNS_Domain name System services, the sender's mail server determines the mail servers for the recipients.

Then, the server opens up a connections to the recipient mail servers and sends the message employing a process similar to that used by the originating client, delivering the message to the recipients.

PGP pretty good privacy

PGP provides confidentiality by encrypting messages to be transmitted or knowledge files to be hold on victimization associate cryptography rule.

Email message is protected by victimization cryptography in numerous ways in which

1.   Signing an email message to ensure its integrity and confirm the identity of its sender.

2.   Encrypting the body of an email message to ensure its confidentiality.

3.   Encrypting the communications between mail servers to protect the confidentiality of both message body and message header.

The first 2 methods, message signing and message body encryption, are often used together.

However, encrypting the transmissions between mail servers is usually used only 2 organizations wish to safeguard emails frequently sent between one another.

For example, organizations may establish a VPN virtual non-public network to encipher the communications between their mail servers over the web.

In contrast to ways that may solely encipher a message body, a VPN will encipher entire messages, together with email header info like senders, recipients, and subjects.

In some cases, organizations might have to safeguard header info.

However, a VPN resolution alone cannot offer a message linguistic communication mechanism, nor will it offer protection for email messages on the complete route from sender to recipient.

MIME   Multipurpose   Internet   Mail Extension

Multi - purpose internet mail extensions transform non-ASCII data at the sender's site to Network Virtual Terminal (NVT) ASCII data.

THEN it delivers it to client's SMTP_simple mail transfer protocol to be sent through the Internet.

The SMTP server at the receiver's side receives the NVT ASCII data and delivers it to MIME to be transformed back to the original non-ASCII data.

MAC message authentication code

MAC could be a cryptography methodology that uses a secret key to encipher a message.

This methodology outputs a raincoat price that may be decrypted by the receiver, victimization constant secret key utilized by the sender.

The Message Authentication Code protects both message's authenticity and data integrity.

Network Layer Security

TCP/ IP protocols may be secured with cryptographic methods and security protocols like IPsec for network layer security, pretty good privacy PGP for emails, and SSL secure sockets layer followed by TLS transport layer security for web traffic.

MFA Multi Factor Authentication

Multi-factor authentication (MFA) could be a methodology of pc access management during which users are granted access solely when with success presenting many separate items of proof to associate authentication mechanism.

Atleast, typically, 2 of the subsequent categories: information (something they know), possession (something they have), and presence (something they are).

Internet resources, like websites and email, is also secured victimization multi-factor authentication.

13 ESSENTIALS

Network security INTER ALIA, includes:

1.   Computer security

2.   Data security

3.   Hardware security

4.   Software security

5.   Information security

6.   Internet security

7.   Automotive security

8.   Network warfare

9.   Mobile security

10.   Cloud security

Computer networking is that the follow of interfacing 2 or additional computing devices with one another for the aim of sharing information.

They are built with a combination of hardware and software.

Here I focuses on wireless networking and computer networks, which is related, but quite different, from social networking.

Computer Network Classification and Area Networks.

Computer networks are often classified in many other ways.

One approach defines the kind of network in keeping with the geographical region it spans.

LANs, ie., local area networks, for example, typically span a single home, school, or small office building.

WANs, Wide Area Networks reach across cities, states, or even across the world.

 The world's largest public WAN is the internet.

Network Design

Computer networks also differ in their design approach.

The two basic forms of network design are called peer –to – peer and client server.

Client-server networks feature centralized server computers that store email, Web pages, files and or applications accessed by shopper computers and different shopper devices.

On a peer-to-peer network, conversely, all devices tend to support constant functions.

Client-server networks are far more common in business.

Peer-to-peer networks additional common in homes.

Network topology defines its layout or structure from the purpose of read of knowledge flow.

In supposed bus networks, for instance, all of the computers share and communicate across one common passage.

In star network, all information flows through one centralized device.

Common kinds of network topologies embrace bus, star, ring networks, and mesh networks.

Network Protocols

Communication languages utilized by pc devices are known as network protocols.

Yet another thanks to classify pc networks is that the set of protocols they support.

Networks typically implement multiple protocols

with every supporting specific application.

Common protocols embrace TCP/IP - the one most typically found on the net and in home networks.

Hardware/software

Special purpose communication devices as well as network routers, access points, and network cables physically glue a network along.

Network operational systems and different code applications generate network traffic and change users to try to helpful things.

Home Computer Networking

While different kinds of networks are designed and maintained by engineers, home networks belong to normal owners, folks typically with very little or no technical background.

Numerous makers turn out broadband router hardware designed to modify home network setup.

A home router allows devices in several rooms to with efficiency share a broadband net association, helps folks to additional simply share their files and printers inside the network, and improves overall network security.

Home networks have inflated in capability with every generation of latest technology.

Years ago, folks unremarkably discovered their home network simply to attach a number of PCs, share some documents and maybe a printer.

Now it is common for households to additionally network game consoles, digital video recorders, and smartphones for streaming sound and video.

Home automation systems have also existed for many years, but these have grown in popularity more recently with practical systems for controlling lights, digital thermostats, and appliances, as well.

Business Computer Networks

SOHO_Small and home office environments use similar technology as found in home networks.

Businesses typically have extra communication,

information storage, and security needs that need increasing their networks in several ways in which, notably because the business gets larger.

A home network usually functions collectively computer network, a business network tends to contain multiple LANs.

Companies with buildings in multiple locations utilize wide-area networking to attach these branch offices along.

Voice over IP communication and network storage and backup technologies are prevalent in businesses, but though available, used by only some households.

Larger companies also maintain their own internal Web sites, called intranets to help with employee business communication.

Networking and the Internet

The popularity of computer networks sharply increased with the creation of the WWW, world wide web, in the 1990s.

Public Web sites, peer to peer (P2P) file sharing

systems, and various other services run on Internet servers across the world.

Wired vs. Wireless Computer Networking

Many of constant protocols like TCP/IP add each wired and wireless networks.

Networks with LAN cables predominated in businesses, schools, and houses for many decades.
WiFi has emerged because the most popular possibility for building new pc networks, partly to support smartphones.

Therefore, the different new types of wireless gadgets that have triggered the increase of mobile networking.

14 ZERO TRUST SECURITY

Zero Trust could be a comprehensive approach to securing all access across your networks, applications, and surroundings.

It protects your personnel, workloads, and geographical point.

Assume zero trust once somebody or one thing requests access to figure assets.

You must first verify their trustworthiness before granting access.

Why zero trust?

The Zero Trust security framework helps you stop unauthorized access, contain breaches, and cut back the danger of an attacker's lateral movement through your network.

With a lot of users, devices, and connections than ever across your network, applications, and within the cloud, however are you able to make sure that the proper access is granted to each?

Increased attack surface

Having a lot of users, devices (including IoT), applications, and servers expands your network perimeter.

How can you exert control and reduce your overall attack surface?

Gaps in visibility

Your network has devices, users, wireless, and different connections.

Meanwhile, your applications, servers, and databases and unit all rebuke one another.

How are you able to gain insight into potential security gaps?

Better secure access across your applications and surroundings, from any user, device, and site.

Zero Trust helps defend your personnel, workloads, and geographic point.
Zero Trust permits you to:

1. Systematically enforce policy-based controls.

2. Gain visibility into users, devices, components, and a lot of across your entire surroundings.

3. Get detailed logs, reports, and alerts that can help you better detect and respond to threats.

It provides more secure access, protect against gaps in visibility, and reduce your attack surface with Zero Trust.

Zero trust for the workforce

It secures your workforce.

Zero Security helps protect your users and their devices against stolen credentials, phishing, and other identity-based attacks.

User Devices

Gain device visibility and establish trust with end point health and management standing.

Applications

Enforce access policies for every app with adaptive and role-based access controls.

Tetration

Tetration secures workloads.

Secure your hybrid, multicloud workloads and contain lateral movement with application segmentation from Tetration.

Get complete visibility and verify the dependencies among databases and applications.

Visibility into workloads

Gain visibility into what's running and what's

vital by distinctive workloads and imposing policies.

Security alerts

Alert or block communication if policy is desecrated by unendingly observance and responding to indicators of compromise.

Zero trust for workplace.

SD-Access secures your workplace.

SDA_Software Defined Access gives insight into users and devices.

It identifies threats and maintain control over all connections across your network, including Internet of Things (IoT) devices like cameras, manufacturing equipment, heart pumps, and more.

Network access

Grant the proper level of network access to users and devices with network authentication.

Network segmentation

Classify and section users, devices, and applications on your network with network segmentation.

Contain threats and contain infected endpoints and revoke network access by unendingly observance and responding to threats.

In addition, Zero Trust integrates with different product to produce complete zero-trust security for any enterprise surroundings.

Advanced Malware Protection (AMP)

Protect your endpoints, network and email with AMP.

Get deep visibility into network and end point threats, and block and take away malware.

Umbrella

Get visibility to protect Internet access across all devices on your network, all office locations, and roaming users.

Next-generation firewalls

With deep network and security visibility, you'll be able to observe and stop threats quick before they reach your personnel, workloads, and geographic point.

AnyConnect provides secure access to the personnel and geographic point, moreover as a lot of insight into user and end point behavior across your entire enterprise.

Email Security

Defend against knowledge loss and inscribe sensitive data with Email Security to shield against phishing, business email compromise, and ransomware.

Unified device management and management of mobile and desktop devices, granting seamless onboarding and automatic application of security policies.

ACI

Application-Centric Infrastructure permits for consistent, policy-based automation for property and segmentation across on-premises and cloud.

Detect and respond Stealthwatch.

Find out WHO is on your network and what they're doing network infrastructure.Detect threats and respond to them quickly with a scalable solution. Automate integrations across Security product to accelerate detection, investigation, and redress
technical partnerships. Build it straightforward to integrate security along with your existing platforms.
Protect and manage platforms and integrate with Microsoft, Symantec, VMware, MobileIron, Jamf, and more.

Integrate with any infrastructure platform, such as Google, Kubernetes, Microsoft Azure, Amazon Web Services (AWS), VMware, and more.

Third Party

Zero Trust security identity suppliers, security information, event management systems, Google, Dell, Ping Identity, Oracle, Okta, Splunk, IBM, etc.

15 FUTURE

Meet the Future of Threat Detection and Response.

The future is bright for network security.

A world is developing in which threat intelligence, advanced data science and automation are readily available to security analysts through elastic, cloud-native applications.

I see the future transformed by ready access to up-to-date machine learning that can detect threats by behavior alone.

It will be a place where security is fortified for all using insights taken from the vast amounts of collective customer data.

The future is a place where our decades of experience on the security frontlines are at our fingertips, along with advanced AI and automation.

It will be a place where security is faster, simpler and more precise.

Apps that uses detectors built on advanced machine learning to help you quickly and precisely detect and respond to threats in our environment are becoming rampant.

Look at how technology can transform security if applied intelligently.

Running a world-class network security system boils down to how quickly you can detect, respond and remediate advanced threats.

Keeping pace with adversaries is a race, and defenders are falling behind more each day.

To regain the edge, network security leaders must evolve toward a new approach to combining human and machine intelligence.

Can you See 2030?

So, what will the longer term look like? largely, it's promising.

Both the tools and therefore the motivation to secure networks are getting progressively out there.

In fact, once you take into account the expansion rate of broadband in terms of shoppers against the expansion of cybercrime, it looks that network operators are gaining ground for many years.

Sturdy network authentication and authorization can make the most this trend.

However, network security can stay difficult.

The value of our networks will continue to grow; we will use them in increasingly interesting ways.

There will continue to be a drive to subvert the network for nefarious purposes.

The dynamic tension between network engineering and network security can continue. Network operators can still perform business in adversarial setting.

The requirement for network security can still be driven by attributes.

The 10g platform **goes to** **supply** reliable service.

As the cable **trade** embarks on **the** **event** of 10G services, **there's plenty of labor** ahead.
We tend to have a robust foundation of **expertise** and technology.

The 10 G goal is **regarding** performance.

But it **should accompany** low **price, prime** **quality,** and **sufficient reliableness**.

10G services **ought** **to** be **straightforward to** **put in dependably, stay** stable and **strong** against cable plant variations and conditions.
Supply service flexibility to **stay** reliable **underneath** a broad set of use cases.

See A Super Highway in Many Directions

Because of this strong reliability foundation in cable technologies, we can build our 10G future with reliability in mind.

Rather than **merely** extending our boundaries and hoping that our existing **ways** to assure reliable services **aresufficient** , **we** **will outline** solutions that bring **dependability** with them.

By focusing **at the same time** on **augmented** performance, lower operational **prices**, and reliable services, **we willevolve** into **a good**, **fascinating** 10G future for **the planet**.

Also, by thoughtfully **selecting** the technologies to develop, **we** **will produce** opportunities **to boost dependability whereas** developing 10G.

Network security includes internet security and computer security related not only to internet but also involves browser security, search engine security, world wide web security, cloud storage security and human element security in addition to operating systems and other applications as a whole.

The objective is to establish rules and measures to use against attacks over the Internet.

Otherwise internet is an unsecure channel for information exchange involving high risk of intrusion and fraud.

Current focus is hindrance the maximum amount as potential on real time protection against acknowledge and new threats.

Threats

1.   Computer crime
2.   Application Vulnerabilities
3.   Eavesdropping
4.   Malware, ie., malicious software
5.   Spyware
6.   Ransomware
7.   Trojans
8.   Viruses
9.   Worms
10.   Rootkits
11.   Bootkits
12.   Keyloggers
13.   Screen scrapers
14.   Exploits
15.   Backdoors
16.   Logic bombs
17.   Payloads
18.   Denial of service
19.   Web shells

Defenses

1.   Computer access control
2.   Application security
3.   Antivirus software
4.   Secure coding
5.   Secure by default
6.   Secure by design
7.   Secure operating systems
8.   Authentication
9.   Multi-factor authentication
10.   Authorization
11.   Data-centric security
12.   Encryption
13.   Firewall
14.   Intrusion detection system IDS
15.   Mobile secure gateway
16.   RASP=Runtime   application   self-protection

Remedies

1.   Network layer security
2.   IPSec- Internet protocol security
3.   Multifactor automation
4.   Security token

5.   Email security [PGP pretty good privacy, MIME multipurpose internet mail extensions, MAC message authentication code]

6.   Firewall [packet filter, SPI stateful packet inspection, applications level gateway]

7.   Browser choice

8.   Internet security products like Antivirus, password managers, VPN, security suites]

9.   Cloud computing security

10.   Network security standards

11.   DLPS data loss prevention software

12.   Time line of computer security hacker history.

ABOUT THE AUTHOR

Aiswarya Ram is the author of the book "CYBER SECURIY". She is MBA in Information Systems and has CCNA in Network security.